CAMERA
ABOVE
THE CLOUDS
Volume 3

CAMERA ABOVE THE CLOUDS

Volume 3

The Colour Collection
of Charles E. Brown

Edited by Anthony Harold

Airlife

England

Photographs Copyright © 1992 Royal Air Force Museum
Text Copyright © 1992 Royal Air Force Museum
First published in the UK in 1992 by
Airlife Publishing Ltd.

British Library Cataloguing in Publication Data
A catalogue record for this book
is available from the British Library

ISBN 1 85310 369 1

Printed by Kyodo Printing Co. (S'pore) pte.

Airlife Publishing Ltd.

101 Longden Road, Shrewsbury, SY3 9EB, England.

Foreword

by Dr Michael A. Fopp, M.A., F.M.A., F.B.I.M., Director
Royal Air Force Museum

Like so many youngsters, who grew up in the immediate post-war years, my interest in aviation was sparked by a number of interlinking factors which conspired to ensure a life-long passion. My school days were spent poring over aviation books, magazines, fashioning rubber-powered flying machines made of balsa wood and tissue paper, and occasionally looking skywards to catch a glimpse of an aeroplane as it flew off to who knows where. Searching the sky fired the imagination; model building was, inevitably, disappointing; only reading books or magazines came near to slaking the thirst to fly. It was many years later that I found out who had provided me with the images which had made such an impression on my youth.

The Royal Air Force Museum acquired the collection of photographs by Charles Brown in 1978, primarily as a result of the interest shown by Tony Harold, one of the Museum's curators. Tony and I had been to the same school and treasured the same dreams. When I joined the Museum in 1979 Tony took little time to show me the source of our schoolboy daydreams by showing me that most of the images which had fired our enthusiasm for aviation had been taken by Charles Brown. The collection was yet to be catalogued and comprised box after box of glass negatives, but Tony was adamant that the treasure should quickly be made available to the public. With characteristic endeavour the first volume of "Camera Above the Clouds" came out in 1983 and Tony Harold's text drew attention to, perhaps, the greatest aviation photographs of all time.

In 1985 Volume II was published with yet more images from the Museum's collection of Charles Brown photographs. This was also the year that I moved on to direct the London Transport Museum in Covent Garden. One of the first images which struck my eye was a 1930's poster of a small boy talking to a train driver of the Southern Railway. Investigation revealed that this, too, was the work of Charles Brown.

In 1988 I returned to the Royal Air Force Museum as Director and found that Tony Harold, now Keeper of Visual Arts, was selecting photographs for a third volume. This was to be an illustrated catalogue of the Charles Brown colour photographs, so that even more images could be made available to a wide audience. His work on the book was stopped by the enormous pressures put on all the Museum staff to record properly in 1990 the 50th Anniversary of the Battle of Britain. In 1991 he died. Tony was killed whilst flying a replica Nieuport in a rehearsal for an airshow. His friends at Hendon and at Airlife were determined to complete the task he had begun. Andy Renwick, Curator of Photographs, compiled the descriptive captions and wrote the Introduction about the photographer and his work. This book is as much a tribute to Tony Harold's years of work for the Museum as it is to the photographs of Charles E. Brown. For those of us who read the book the images repeat a powerful reminder of the excellence of Charles Brown's photography. For those of us who knew Tony Harold the book will bring back memories of a gentle man and good friend.

Introduction

Unlike his two contemporaries, John Yoxall of *Flight* and Charles Sims of *The Aeroplane*, Charles Brown worked as a freelance photographer. This gave him many more opportunities to sell his photographs as he was not tied to one publisher. One regular user was the magazine *Aeronautics* which had been founded as *Popular Flying* by W.E. Johns in 1932.

In the USA there existed a similar magazine, *Flying*, which was founded, edited and published by William B. Ziff. In September 1942 they published a special Royal Air Force issue for which they required colour photographs of the RAF in action in addition to text.

The Air Ministry played a central role in the production of the special issue of *Flying*, liaising with the Ministry of Information to compile the text. This had to be assembled at the Air Ministry before 1 May, 1942, and sent to America no later than 1 July, 1942.

At the outbreak of World War II Brown was offered a post at the Air Ministry but he declined it, preferring to remain freelance and thus assist both the Air Ministry and the Admiralty for whom he also often worked. He did, however, maintain a good relationship with the Air Ministry and his services were often used by them.

Colour film was unavailable in Britain during the war but William Ziff was able to supply 35mm Kodachrome film. For many press photographers, used to working only with plate cameras, this would have been a problem but Charles Brown had been using a 35mm Zeiss Contax camera since 1935. Using this camera he took colour photographs which were published in the special edition of *Flying*.

The colour film had to be sent to the USA for processing and approval by William Ziff. Thus it had to be correct first time and Charles Brown could not afford to make mistakes for it would be impossible to repeat the shot. The difficulty of obtaining supplies also meant that he had to avoid taking too many exposures of the same subject.

The connection with the USA continued through the war with Charles Brown becoming an accredited war correspondent with both the American and British forces. He was able to follow the Allies' progress from France to Germany after the D-Day landings. This liaison with the Americans was probably another useful source of colour film stock.

After the war colour film gradually became more readily available, not just in 35mm but also as sheet film which would fit Brown's Zeiss Palmos plate camera. His work for the British aircraft industry continued but now, in addition to his usual black-and-white work, he was able to include colour photographs. As in wartime, Charles Brown continued to be frugal in his use of colour film. He averaged only thirty colour transparencies per year – a very small proportion of his total output.

It is worthy of note that he used colour film mainly for aeronautical subjects. Despite the fact that he is best known for his photographs of aircraft he had always covered a variety of topics and continued to do so until his semi-retirement. It was rare, however, that he used colour on other subjects: nautical subjects are those which feature most often.

Much of his post-war colour work was taken in September at the SBAC displays at Farnborough. Many of the aircraft manufacturers and aviation publishers wanted new images of the latest aircraft types for publication, often turning to Charles Brown for the photographs necessary to fulfil their needs. Sadly, many of the aircraft failed to enter production but Charles Brown was at least able to preserve photographs of them.

It was the predominance of black-and-white within the publishing world which led Charles Brown to continue in the medium he knew best. Much of his skill came not just in his camera work but also in his work in the darkroom. Colour photography removed the personal aspect from his work.

The development of colour transparency film in the darkroom without the need to send it to a particular laboratory only became possible after Charles Brown retired. Similarly, the overall quality of colour film has improved sufficiently to allow it now to dominate monochrome in the publishing world. Colour film is now considered by many to be more versatile and easier to use than monochrome, a reversal of the situation in which Charles Brown found himself.

Most of the photographs that have survived from World War Two are black-and-white because colour stock deteriorates much more rapidly. It is fortunate that this remarkable heritage, now owned by the the RAF Museum, has survived for us to admire and enjoy for many years to come.

CAMERA ABOVE THE CLOUDS

Volume 3

The Colour Collection

A Bristol Beaufort I of No. 217 Squadron. Designed as a torpedo-bomber, the type entered RAF service in November 1939 with Coastal Command. It also operated in the Middle East and with the Royal Australian Air Force.
P100079

The Fleet Air Arm operated navalised versions of both the Spitfire and Hurricane – the Supermarine Seafire and the Hawker Sea Hurricane. These aircraft differed from the land-based versions by having arrester hooks and folding wings to enable them to operate from aircraft carriers.

P100592

The first squadron to operate the type, No. 35 Squadron, took part in many famous bombing raids with the Handley Page Halifax. This well known study is of a Halifax B.II Series I of the squadron which was shot down on the night of 28/29 August 1942.
P100317

While the Fleet Air Arm was waiting for its Seafires to be delivered,
a number of Spitfires from the RAF were used to provide training.
These are Spitfire Ia aircraft from No. 761 Training Squadron.
P100605

Avro Lancaster B.I bombers on 20 June 1942, shortly after they had
replaced the Avro Manchesters in No. 207 Squadron.
P100024

Unlike the other versions of the Hawker Sea Hurricane, the Mk.Ia had no arrester hook having been adapted for use on Catapult Armed Merchant (CAM) ships. If enemy aircraft threatened a convoy, the defending aircraft would be catapulted from a CAM-ship to intercept and then ditched after the sortie.
P100386

The lack of power in the Allison V-1710 engine of the North American Mustang I resulted in the type being used for reconnaissance and ground attack. When the Rolls-Royce Merlin was fitted the Mustang became one of the great fighter aircraft of World War II.
P100496

A train of twenty-four 500lb (227kg) bombs is delivered to a Short Stirling I of 1651 HCU at RAF Waterbeach on 29 April 1942. It was from the Heavy Conversion Units that crews were posted to operational squadrons after a period of training and operational flying.
P100558

This Supermarine Spitfire Vb of No. 222 Squadron, RAF North
Weald, carries the pennant of Squadron Leader R. M. Milne who
commanded the squadron until May 1942.
P100601

The Empire Central Flying School was formed in 1942 to ensure that instructors destined for any of the flying schools throughout the Empire were aware of the latest tactics and had flown the latest aircraft types. Shown here are two Supermarine Spitfires IIa and a Hawker Hurricane I of the ECFS
P100360

Avro Lancaster B.III (ED592) was built in Manchester, the home of
the Avro company. Charles Brown had his opportunity to photograph
it during a test flight before it was delivered to a squadron.
P100026

17

Formed at Quonset, USA, No. 846 Squadron was the first to operate the Grumman Avenger I in home waters. While escorting a convoy to Russia in April 1944 the squadron shared in the destruction of two U-boats.

P100312

The Fairey Barracuda had a prolonged entry into Naval service. First designed in 1937, the prototype did not fly until 1940 and the type did not enter operational service until 1943 as a replacement for the Fairey Albacore. Only twenty-five of the Barracuda Mk.I shown below were built.
P100186

It was intended that the Hawker Typhoon should enter service as an interceptor fighter in July 1940. Problems with the Napier Sabre engine, however, delayed its entry into service until 1941 when it became the first RAF aircraft capable of flying at 400mph (644km/h)
P100407

The lack of performance at altitude prevented the Hawker Typhoon from being one of the great fighters of the Second World War. It was to excel, however, in the ground attack role against enemy tanks and railways.
P100408

The Percival Proctor was used both as a communications aircraft and as a wireless trainer. This prototype Proctor IV differed from earlier versions by having four seats, dual controls and a longer, deeper, fuselage. The Proctor IV was used at Hendon for many years in its communications role.
P100504

The Supermarine Spitfire PR.XI was the main reconnaissance version to be powered by the Rolls-Royce Merlin. The range of this unarmed aircraft could be extended to 2,000 miles (3220km) by the use of a detachable belly tank.
P100606

The Vickers Warwick was designed as a bomber but entered service
in the air-sea rescue role. With a range of 2,300 miles (3700km), the
Warwick I was capable of dropping an airborne lifeboat to ditched
aircrew many miles from shore.
P100684

A famous study of the Vickers Wellington Ia. This aircraft was photographed while it served with the Central Gunnery School. Note that only the rear turret is equipped with its two .303 Browning machine guns. It was later converted to become a Wellington XV and served with Transport Command.
P100695

Although sixty-seven aircraft were ordered and built for the RAF, no Westland Welkin I high altitude fighter entered squadron service.
P100704

Designed and first flown in 1942, the Avro York was ordered as a transport aircraft for the RAF. In 1944, however, five were diverted to BOAC in whose wartime markings the first was photographed on 14 January 1944.
P100044

Converted from a Fairey Firefly F.I, this is the prototype Firefly FR.4 after it had been modified to the final production specification. A total of 160 were built including forty for the Royal Netherlands Naval Air Service.
P100261

Developed from the Tipsy M, only two Fairey Primer prototypes
were built at Hamble.
P100227

Developed from the Hawker Typhoon, the Hawker Tempest V was the main production version to use the Napier Sabre engine and closely resembled its predecessor. It was also the only version of the Tempest to see action during World War II, accounting for 638 V1 flying bombs and at least eleven Me262 jet fighters.
P100390

Capable of carrying a seven ton (7,100kg) tank, the Hamilcar was
designed by General Aircraft Ltd. Used in both the Normandy and
Arnhem landings the Hamilcars are seen at Tarrant Rushton in
November 1944. The gliders were towed by Handley Page Halifax
aircraft, examples of which can be seen in the background.
P100276

The Gloster Meteor was the first jet aircraft to enter squadron service with the RAF. The Meteor F.4 shown was fitted with the Rolls-Royce Derwent V of 3,500lb thrust (15.57kN), nearly twice the power of the Rolls Royce Welland fitted in the Meteor F.I used in World War II.

P100283

Martin B-26B Marauder "Dee-Feater" of the 496 BS, 497 BG,
USAAF, August 1944.
P100470

The Northrop P-61A was designed for use as a night-fighter and not
converted to the role as were several other types.
P100497

Problems with the Rolls-Royce Peregrine engines prevented the
Westland Whirlwind from fulfilling its true potential. Only two
squadrons were formed, but used the long range of the aircraft to
good effect as bomber escorts and in the ground attack role. It was
replaced in 1943 by the Hawker Typhoon.
P100707

Although designed during World War II, the De Havilland Vampire F.1 entered RAF service in 1946. Initial production was undertaken by English Electric at Preston with test flying at Salmesbury from where this example was flying.
P1000172

OPPOSITE
The Blackburn Firebrand was originally designed in 1939 as an interceptor but did not enter service until 1945 having been modified as a torpedo-carrying strike fighter. This aircraft was the first production Firebrand TF.4, of which 102 were built.
P100189

It was originally planned to use the Hawker Tempest II in the Far East but the surrender of Japan occurred before its deployment. Powered by a Bristol Centaurus radial engine, the Tempest II finally saw action in 1948 against Malayan terrorists.
P100394

The Supermarine Spiteful was intended as a replacement for the
Spitfire. The end of World War II caused the cancellation of orders
and only seventeen were completed, none entering service. A
Spiteful XIV is shown.
P100597

Many bomber aircraft were adapted as transport aircraft after the war. The Handley Page Halifax was no exception. The Halifax C.VIII was built as a freighter with interior accommodation for eleven passengers and a detachable pannier under the fuselage for an additional 8,000lbs (3,629kg) of freight.
P100323

Ordered as a Sunderland replacement, the end of World War II led to
the cancellation of the Short Shetland I after the prototype had flown,
despite its good handling characteristics.
P100549

In addition to intercepting V1 flying bombs, the Rolls-Royce Griffon-powered Supermarine Spitfire XIV served with the 2nd Tactical Air Force. Flying from airfields liberated on the Continent it used its ability to fly at 44,500 feet (13.6km) to provide high-altitude defence for the Allied forces.
P100609

Developed from the Wellington, the Vickers Viking 1 was used by
BEA. After using the Viking the RAF ordered a military version, the
Valetta.

P100647

Boeing B-17G Flying Fortress 'A bit o' lace' of the 709 BS, 447 BG, USAAF, over England after completing eighty-three bombing missions.
P100063

An Avro Lancastrian III flying on the power of two Rolls-Royce
Nene jet engines which have replaced the two outer Rolls-Royce
Merlins on this engine test-bed, 24 September 1946.
P100037

The Miles Messenger was originally designed and built during World War II as a communications aircraft, production continuing after the war for civilian buyers. The Miles Messenger 3 was a post-war development which featured fully retractable flaps and dual control, but only two were built.
P100483

Designed to replace the Avro York, the Handley Page Hastings operated alongside it during the Berlin Airlift. This first Hastings prototype made its maiden flight on 7 May 1946, only weeks before it was photographed by Charles Brown.

P100327

47

48

Powered by Rolls-Royce Griffon engines, the later marks of Supermarine Spitfire received a new wing replacing the famous elliptical wing.
P100613

The Percival Prentice was designed as a replacement for the venerable Tiger Moth. This prototype first flew on 31 March 1946. It was modified to the more familiar configuration as a result of test flying.
P100499

These Fairey Barracuda TR.III aircraft of No. 744 Squadron, Fleet Air Arm, gained a rare distinction. The type was relegated to training in 1946 but in 1947 re-entered operational service with No. 815 Squadron.
P100188

Many aircraft have been converted to operate as target-tugs but the Miles Martinet I was designed from the beginning to fulfil that role. Over 1700 of these wooden aircraft were built by Miles Aircraft at Woodley.
P100481

The Bristol Brigand TF.1 had only a brief career as a torpedo-bomber before being converted to a land-bomber, serving in Iraq, Aden and Malaya.
P100082

The first unit of the Fleet Air Arm to receive the De Havilland Sea
Hornet F.20 was No. 801 Squadron at RNAS Ford in July 1947.
Three aircraft from that squadron are seen here in September of that
year.
P100161

A De Havilland Sea Mosquito TR.33 of No. 771 Squadron, Fleet Air Arm, on 27 October 1947.
P100166

Registered in Belgium, this Ercoupe was photographed on 11 May
1947. Built by the Engineering and Research Corporation of the
USA after World War II, the type was originally marketed in 1940.
P100185

The Miles Aerovan 1 was capable of carrying eight passengers or
one ton (1,016kg) of freight, including small cars.
P100471

A popular post-war aeroplane, most Miles Geminis were sold for export.
P100479

The Tipsy Belfair was built in the UK after World War II, developed
from the pre-war Tipsy B which had been designed and built in
Belgium.
P100625

The De Havilland Sea Hornet F.20 was used as a long range ship-borne fighter. The prototype, seen here during deck landing trials on HMS Ocean, did not have folding wings – unlike the production aircraft.
P100160

After World War II the Avro Lancaster was re-designed for use as a transport aircraft. This new version was named the Avro Lancastrian. These, of Skyways Ltd, were used to fly fuel oils to Berlin during the airlift in 1947 and 1948.
P100027

The Saunders Roe SR.A/1 was the world's only jet powered flying boat. Only prototypes were built before advances in conventional aircraft design rendered the concept obsolete.
P100523

The Avro Anson T.20 was built for flying training in Southern Rhodesia. The transparent nose enabled this version to be used for the training of all aircrew, including bomb-aimers.
P100017

Powered by an Armstrong Siddeley Mamba turboprop, the Avro
Athena T.1 was ordered to replace North American Harvard
advanced trainers. The production version, the Athena T.2 was re-
engined with a Rolls-Royce Merlin but only eleven were ordered,
serving mainly with the RAF Flying College at Manby.
P100019

An early post-war airliner, this Avro Tudor IV of British South American Airways was used between London and Bermuda before being converted for use as a freighter.
P100042

Chrislea CH.3 Super Ace on 19 August 1948. Only twenty-six of these aircraft were completed at Exeter by this company.
P100129

The De Havilland D.H.108 Swallow was designed to break the sound barrier. In September 1948 this example became the first British aircraft to exceed the speed of sound.
P100142

The classic photograph of the Avro Lancaster; PP267 on a test flight from Castle Bromwich.
P100233

RNAS Eglinton was the home for these Fairey Firefly FR.4 aircraft
of No. 816 Squadron and Hawker Sea Furys of No. 805 Squadron
Royal Australian Navy. Both squadrons later took part in the Korean
War.
P100206

Three Gloster Meteor III aircraft were fitted with the uprated Rolls-Royce Derwent V jet engines and arrester hooks. Supplied to the Royal Navy they were then used for deck landing trials on HMS Implacable.
P100296

By the time Charles Brown took this photograph at Horsham St Faith, RAF fighters had their camouflage replaced by a silver high-speed finish. These Gloster Meteor F.4 aircraft equipped No. 245 and No. 263 Squadrons, the first to use this version.
P100298

The Hawker P.1040 was initially designed for the RAF. It was converted, however, for use by the Royal Navy as the Sea Hawk. The first P.1040 is shown.
P100364

The Short Solent 3 was converted on the production line from the
Short Seaford which had originally been ordered for the RAF. This
aircraft served with BOAC.
P100550

The Supermarine Seagull was the last of the line which began with
the original Seagull of the 1920s. Intended for the air-sea rescue role
it was rendered obsolete by the development of the helicopter.
P100595

Boeing KB-29M Superfortress of the USAF refuelling a Gloster Meteor F.4 of the Refuelling Trials Flight, with Gloster Meteor F.8 aircraft of No. 245 Squadron on either side. The USAF eventually standardised on the "flying boom" method of refuelling aircraft in flight instead of the probe-and-drogue method illustrated.
P100303

An unusual engine arrangement was used in the Fairey Gyrodyne. A single 550hp (410kW) Alvis Leonides engine drove a two bladed tractor propeller in the starboard wing stub and the rotor. On 28 June 1948, flown by Squadron Leader Basil Arkell, the Fairey Gyrodyne established a new world speed record for helicopters of 124.3mph (200km/h).

P100224

Designed to the same specification as the Vickers Viscount, the
Armstrong Whitworth Apollo, powered by four Armstrong Siddeley
Mamba turboprops, failed to attract orders.
P100005

The Boeing 377 Stratocruiser was used by BOAC on the London-New York route during the 1950s. The first is seen here in November 1949.
P100071

De Havilland Mosquito FB.6 of No. 334 Squadron, Norwegian Air
Force, in June 1949.
P100158

OPPOSITE
The Hawker Sea Fury T.20 was based upon a version ordered by the
Iraqi Air Force. Unlike the single-seat version the Sea Fury T.20 had
no arrester hook and could not operate from aircraft carriers.
P100381

This first production Short Sealand flew for the first time on 1 August 1949. It was written off, however, in October 1949 in a flying accident in Norway.
P100545

The De Havilland Comet 1 prototype shown here was the first airliner to fly powered by turbojets. Test pilot John Cunningham made the famous flight on 27 July 1949.
P100417

The Vickers Varsity was ordered to replace Vickers Wellingtons and Valettas used for training. Pilots, navigators and bomb aimers were all trained on this aircraft. The pannier was fitted with a window for bomb-aiming and accommodation for twenty-four 25lb (11.4kg) practice bombs.
P100640

The Vickers Valetta C.1 replaced the Douglas Dakota in RAF service and was used in a variety of transport roles. This early production version is seen over Southampton Docks.
P100628

Descended from the Avro Lancaster, the Avro Shackleton MR.1 was
built as its replacement in RAF Coastal Command. The dome under
the nose housed an air-to-surface radar.
P100447

De Havilland Canada Beaver G-ALOW on 2 April 1950. Designed in Canada, the type was later purchased by the Army Air Corps as the Beaver AL.1.
P100137

Powered by a Rolls-Royce Avon, the prototype Supermarine Swift first flew on 5 August 1951. Ordered as a safeguard in case of failure by the Hunter, the Swift was beset by problems and entered service with only one fighter unit, No. 56 Squadron. It was successfully developed, however, for tactical reconnaissance.
P100622

The Supermarine Attacker was originally designed for the RAF but entered service with the Fleet Air Arm. This aircraft is from No. 800 Squadron, the first operational Royal Navy jet squadron.
P100586

The United States of America established a lead in the development of the helicopter. Two of the earliest types to be imported into Britain after the war for civil use are shown here, the Bell 47 (nearest) and the Sikorsky S-51.
P100050

The Vickers Valiant was the most conventional of the V-bombers
and was the first to enter service. In addition to its nuclear role, the
type was also used as a conventional bomber, seeing service over
Suez in 1956. The only remaining example is preserved at the RAF
Museum.

P100631

89

RAF Squadrons in Britain visited stations in the Mediterranean each year to take advantage of the good weather, a practice still used by the Red Arrows display team. Personnel are seen here servicing De Havilland Vampire F.3 aircraft of No. 601 Squadron, Royal Auxiliary Air Force, at RAF Ta Kali, Malta, in June 1952.
P100174

Vickers Viscount G-AMAV was the prototype of the 700 series. It was used by BEA in the England New Zealand air race of 1953. P100674

The Bristol Sycamore was the first helicopter designed and built in Britain to enter RAF service. This is a Sycamore HR.14, the last variant produced.
P100112

The English Electric Canberra was the first jet bomber to enter service with the Royal Air Force. This prototype of the training version, the Canberra T.4, later served with No. 231 OCU and No. 16 Squadron, RAF.
P100184

The Bristol 173 was designed to operate airliner feeder services from city centres to airports. The prototype first flew in January 1952 and is seen here in September of that year. Although not used as a civil aircraft it was later developed into the Westland Belvedere for the Royal Air Force.
P100076

OPPOSITE
The Hunting Percival Provost T.1 was the last piston-engined basic trainer to see service with the RAF. The prototype was powered initially with an Armstong Siddeley Cheetah 18 radial engine. It is shown here after being fitted with the Alvis Leonides 126 engine as used in the production aircraft.
P100515

Blackburn Beverley prototype WZ889 is seen here in September 1953, the same year as its first flight. When it entered service it was the largest aircraft in the RAF.
P100055

Gloster Meteor F.8 aircraft and pilots of No. 601 and No. 604
Squadrons, Royal Auxiliary Air Force, at RAF North Weald in 1953.
P100310

Hunting Jet Provost T.1 XD674 was the first of 10 development aircraft delivered to No. 2 FTS at RAF Hullavington. The type was used to prove the feasibility of training pilots on jet aircraft only and became the first jet-powered basic trainer to enter service with the RAF.
P100113

OPPOSITE
Neville Duke with Hawker Hunter WB188. Built as the first prototype, this aircraft was modified to form the sole Mk.3 and as such, with Neville Duke at the controls, set a new world air speed record of 727.63mph (1171km/h) on 7 September 1953.
P100433

Gloster Meteor NF.12 and NF.14 aircraft of No. 152 Squadron in
June 1955. The night-fighter versions of the Meteor were built by
Armstrong Whitworth to allow Glosters to concentrate on the Meteor
F.8 and the Javelin.

P100010

Unlike other versions of the Handley Page Hermes, the Hermes V was fitted with Bristol Theseus turboprops. Only two Mk.Vs were built.
P100336

The Fairey F.D.2 was built as a transonic research aircraft. On 10 March 1956 this aircraft raised the world air speed record to 1,132mph (1,820km/h). It was later modified as the BAC 221 and assisted in the Concorde development programme.
P100192

Powered by an Armstrong Siddeley Double Mamba 100 turboprop,
the prototype Fairey Gannet T.2 trainer was photographed in
September 1955
P100213

The Folland Midge was designed and built as a private venture at Hamble. The type was modified to form the Folland Gnat fighter which was exported and the Folland Gnat trainer which saw service with the RAF. For many years the Gnat was used by the Red Arrows display team.

P100427

The Hawker P.1052 was a version of the P.1040 with swept wings
for use by the Royal Navy. The type was not ordered for the Fleet
Air Arm but it provided valuable research information.
P100370

Scottish Aviation Twin Pioneer prototype. Designed as a sixteen-passenger airliner the type was purchased by the Royal Air Force as a multi-role transport aircraft.
P100529

Avro Lincoln II de-icing test aircraft. The frame in front of the wing
section on the rear fuselage was used to spray water onto the wing in
order to produce ice.
P100040

Powered by four Armstrong Siddeley Sapphire turbojets, the
Handley Page Victor B.1, of which this is the first production
aircraft, entered RAF service with No. 232 OCU at RAF Gaydon in
1957.
P100348

A Convair 340 in July 1956, modified by the replacement of its Pratt and Whitney R-2800 radial piston engines by two Napier Eland turboprops.
P100133

Along with many other firsts, the De Havilland Comet equipped the
world's first jet transport squadron. The first Comet C.2 aircraft were
received by No. 216 Squadron, RAF, in July 1956, one of which is
seen here.
P100419

OPPOSITE
Westland licence-built the Sikorsky S-55 as the Whirlwind. The type
was produced for the RN, RAF, civil customers and for export.
P100708

The Piaggio P.166 differs from many modern aircraft by having
pusher engines and the gull wing.
P100516

The Accountant, which first flew on 9 July 1957, was the only
attempt to design and build an airliner by Aviation Traders
Engineering Ltd. Only this prototype was completed.
P100013

The Hawker Sea Hawk FB.5 aircraft of No. 738 Training Squadron received a special red finish for their display in the 1957 Farnborough show. The team is seen during a rehearsal of their display routine.
P100382

The Fairey Rotodyne prototype, XE521, first flew on 10 April 1958 using an unique arrangement. Two Napier Eland turboprops provided forward thrust and fuel was also burnt at the tips of the rotor blades. Despite initial interest from the RAF, BEA and the USA, the project was cancelled in 1962.
P100267

This first prototype of the Bristol 170 Freighter was converted to Mk.2 Wayfarer specification in 1958. Its flying career lasted from 1945 until 1963.
P100105

116

The English Electric Lightning was the first true British supersonic
fighter. This is the prototype Lightning T.4 two-seat trainer which
first flew on 6 May 1959.
P100117

The Vickers Vanguard was designed as a second generation
turboprop airliner to replace the Vickers Viscount. Most airlines,
however, wanted turbojet aircraft and few buyers could be found.
They were later converted by BEA for use as freighters.
P100637

The Slingsby T.43 Skylark 3 was probably the most successful
Slingsby design, being used to win the 1960 World Gliding
Championship.

P100735

First flown in 1961, Slingsby T.50 Skylark 4 was used to win both
the US and Canadian National Championships.
P100736

The Slingsby T.51 Dart was the last all-wooden high performance glider built by Slingsby. There were two versions, the 15 which had a 49ft (15m) wing span and this version, the 17, which introduced metal components such as the tailplane and had a 56ft (17m) wingspan.
P100740

De Havilland D.H.125 prototype G-ARYA, the first in a long line
of business jets still in production today as the British Aerospace
125-1000.
P100432

122

The Blackburn Buccaneer S.1 was ordered by the Royal Navy as a low level, high speed bomber. The first operational unit to use the type was No. 801 Squadron based at RNAS Lossiemouth and deployed on HMS Ark Royal and HMS Victorious.
P100415

The Hawker P.1127 was the forerunner of the Harrier VTOL jet. The
Bristol Siddeley Pegasus Pg.5 produced only 15,500lbs of thrust
(68.95kN) compared to the 21,750lbs thrust (96.75kN) of the Rolls-
Royce Pegasus 105 used in the British Aerospace Harrier GR.5.
P100446

The 'Pelicans' display team of the RAF Central Flying School taking off from Farnborough in 1962 to perform formation aerobatics at the SBAC show.
P100240

Designed to meet a requirement from BEA, the Hawker Siddeley
H.S.121 Trident 1 entered service in 1964. Its autoland system
enabled it to land in conditions which grounded most other aircraft
types.
P100454

OPPOSITE
The Air Ministry had doubts about the slow-speed handling of the
English Electric Lightning. To investigate this they ordered the Short
S.B.5 seen here, now preserved at the Aerospace Museum, Cosford.
P100541

G-ARXM was the enlarged second prototype of the Beagle B.206, the B.206Y. Intended to compete against the American companies in the 'light executive twin' category, the Basset (as it was named by the RAF) was not very successful and only eighty-five were completed.
P100047

Only ten Short Belfast C.1 transport aircraft were built, all serving with No. 53 Squadron, RAF. Seen here at Farnborough in 1964, the Belfast could carry 80,000lb (36,290kg) of freight or 150 fully equipped troops when it entered service in 1966.
P100537

The RAF ordered three aircraft types to carry Britain's nuclear deterrent. The Handley Page Victor was the last of the three. It was also the fastest and could carry a larger conventional bomb load than the other two.
P100345

130

Abbreviations

AuxAF	Auxiliary Air Force
BEA	British European Airways
BG	Bombardment Group
BOAC	British Overseas Airways Corporation
BS	Bombardment Squadron
CFS	Central Flying School
ECFS	Empire Central Flying School
FAA	Fleet Air Arm
FG	Fighter Group
FTS	Flying Training School
HCU	Heavy Conversion Unit
HMS	Her (His) Majesty's Ship
NFS	Night Fighter Squadron
OCU	Operational Conversion Unit
OTU	Operational Training Unit
RAAF	Royal Australian Air Force
RAF	Royal Air Force
RAuxAF	Royal Auxiliary Air Force
RCAF	Royal Canadian Air Force
RMS	Royal Mail Ship
RNAS	Royal Naval Air Station
SBAC	Society of British Aerospace Constructors
Sqn	Squadron
USAAF	United States Army Air Force
USAF	United States Air Force
VTOL	Vertical take-off and landing

Index

General Aircraft Hamilcar	P100275 – P100277
Universal	P100051 – P100053
Germany: Air Force	P100462
Gloster Meteor	P100009 – P100010, P100278 – P100311,
	P100730 – P100731
Grumman Avenger	P100312 – P100313
Wildcat	P100314 – P100316
Handley Page Halifax	P100317 – P100323
Hampden	P100324 – P100325
Hastings	P100326 – P100329
Hermes	P100335 – P100343
H.P.R.3 Herald	P100330 – P100334
Marathon	P100344
Victor	P100345 – P100359
Hawker Hunter	P100433 – P100445
Hurricane	P100360 – P100363
P.1040	P100364 – P100367
P.1052	P100368 – P100379
P.1127	P100445 – P100446
Sea Fury	P100205 – P100206, P100380 – P100381
Sea Hawk	P100386 – P100388, P100592
Sea Hurricane	P100386 – P100388, P100592
Hawker Tempest	P100389 – P100398, P100762 – P100763
Typhoon	P100399 – P100410
Hawker Siddeley Argosy	See Armstrong Whitworth AW.650 Argosy
Buccaneer	See Blackburn Buccaneer
Comet	See De Havilland DH.106 Comet
Gnat	See Folland Gnat
H.S.125	See De Havilland DH.125
Hunter	See Hawker Hunter
Trident	P100454 – P100455
Hunting Jet Provost	See BAC Jet Provost
Junkers Ju.87	P100462
Ju.88	P100462
KLM	P100680 – P100681
Lockheed Hudson	P100465 – P100467
Martin B-26 Marauder	P100469 – P100470
Middle East Airlines	P100425 – P100426
Miles Aerovan	P100471 – P100475
Gemini	P100477 – P100480
HDM.105	P100476
Martinet	P100481 – P100482
Master	P100468
Messenger	P100483 – P100485
Mitchell-Proctor Kittiwake	P100486 – P100487
Netherlands: Navy	P100202 – P100203
North American Mitchell	P100488 – P100491
Mustang	P100492 – P100495
Northrop P-61 Black Widow	P100497 – P100498
Norway: Air Force: Units	
332 Squadron	P100176 – P100177
334 Squadron	P100158
Operation Plainfare	See Berlin Airlift

Percival Prentice	P100499 – P100501
Prince	P100502 – P100503
Proctor	P100504 – P100512
Provost	P100513 – P100515
Piaggio P.166	P100516 – P100519
Poland: Air Force: Units	
316 Squadron	See Royal Air Force: Units
Republic F-84 Thunderjet	P100069 – P100070
P-47 Thunderbolt	P100520 – P100521
Royal Air Force: Marine Craft	
68' High Speed Launch	P100747 – P100751
Royal Air Force: Stations	
Banff	P100150 – P100153
Beaulieu	P100583
Biggin Hill	P100764 – P100765
Bradwell Bay	P100389
Foulsham	P100488 – P100489
Horsham St. Faith	P100298
Linton on Ouse	P100319
Matlask	P100399 – P100401
Melsbroek	P100157, P100490 – P100491
Mildenhall	P100689 – P100691
North Weald	P100310 – P100311, P100599 – P100600
Odiham	P100170
Sawbridgeworth	P100492 – P100495
Ta Kali	P100174 – P100175, P100309
Tarrant Rushton	P100275 – P100277, P100320
Royal Air Force: Units	
2 Flying Training School	P100114 – P100116
2 Squadron	P100492 – P100495
6 Operational Training Unit	P100465 – P100467
35 Squadron	P100317 – P100319, P100321
47 Squadron	P100237 – P100238
56 Squadron	P100399 – P100401
61 Squadron	P100255 – P100257
87 Squadron	P100362
92 Squadron	P100444
105 Squadron	P100149
109 Squadron	P100255 – P100257
111 Squadron	P100443
140 Squadron	P100157
143 Squadron	P100152 – P100153
152 Squadron	P100009 – P100010
179 Squadron	P100687 – P100688
180 Squadron	P100488 – P100491
207 Squadron	P100021 – P100025
216 Squadron	P100419 – P100424
222 Squadron	P100599 – P100601
230 Squadron	P100579 – P100580
245 Squadron	P100298, P100303 – P100308
247 Squadron	P100170 – P100173
257 Squadron	P100402 – P100407, P100435 – P100442
263 Squadron	P100298

271 Squadron	P100079 – P100081
298 Squadron	P100320
316 Squadron	P100602 – P100604
501 Squadron	P100389
570 Squadron	P100576
571 Squadron	P100154 – P100156
601 Squadron	P100174 – P100175, P100310 –P100311
604 Squadron	P100310 – P100311
611 Squadron	P100764 – P100765
616 Squadron	P100279 – P100280
1651 Heavy Conversion Unit	P100556 – P100575
Airborne Forces Exp. Establishment	P100583
Cambridge University Air Squadron	P100168
Central Flying School	P100240
Central Gunnery School	P100695
Empire Central Flying School	P100360 – P100361
Refuelling Trials Flight	P100303 – P100308
Royal Auxiliary Air Force	See Royal Air Force
RMS Durban Castle	P100169
Royal Navy: Ships	
HMS Bulwark	P100752 – P100756
HMS Eagle	P100588 – P100590
HMS Implacable	P100296 – P100297, P100577 – P100578
	P100757
HMS Ocean	P100159 – P100160
HMS Searcher	P100314 – P100316
Royal Navy: Stations	
Yeovilton	P100468, P100591 – P100592
Royal Navy: Units	
744 Squadron	P100188
760 Squadron	P100386 – P100388, P100468,
	P100591 – P100592
761 Squadron	P100207, P100605
771 Squadron	P100166
800 Squadron	P100586 – P100590
801 Squadron	P100161 – P100165, P100415
813 Squadron	P100716
824 Squadron	P100216
846 Squadron	P100312 – P100313
882 Squadron	P100314 – P100316
Saunders Roe Princess	P100526
SR.A/1	P100522 – P100525
Sayer, P. E. G.	P100763
Scottish Aviation Twin Pioneer	P100527 – P100536
Short Belfast	P100537 – P100538
S.B.5	P100539 – P100541
S.C.1	P100542 – P100544
Sealand	P100545 – P100547
Shetland	P100548 – P100549
Solent	P100550 – P100555
Stirling	P100556 – P100576
Sturgeon	P100577 – P100578

Sunderland	P100579 – P100582
Sikorsky Hoverfly II	P100583
S-51	P100049 – P100050
S-58	P100706
Skyways	P100027
Slingsby T.25 Gull 4	P100732
T.41 Skylark 2	P100733
T.43 Skylark 3G	P100735
T.45 Swallow	P100734
T.49 Capstan	P100738 – P100739
T.50 Skylark 4	P100736 – P100737
T.51 Dart 17	P100740 – P100743
Sperry Gyroscope Company	P100014 – P100015
Standard Austria	P100744 – P100746
Supermarine 510	P100584 – P100585
Attacker	P100586 – P100590
Seafire	P100591 – P100593
Seagull	P100594 – P100595
Spiteful	P100596 – P100598
Spitfire	P100360 – P100361, P100599– P100619,
P100764 – P100765	
Swift	P100620 – P100623
Tipsy Belfair	P100625 – P100626
Trainer	P100624
Trans Canada Airlines	P100638 – P100639
USA: Army Air Force: Units	
56 Fighter Group	P100520 – P100521
397 Bombardment Group	P100469 – P100470
422 Night Fighter Squadron	P100497 – P100498
447 Bombardment Group	P100063 – P100068, P100723 – P100728
596 Bombardment Squadron	P100469 – P100470
709 Bombardment Squadron	P100063 – P100068, P100723 – P100728
Vickers Valetta	P100630 – P100636
Valiant	P100627 – P100629
Vanguard	P100637 – P100639
Varsity	P100640 – P100644
Viking	P100645 – P100664
Viking (Nene)	P100665 – P100667
Viscount	P100668 – P100681
Warwick	P100682 – P100688
Wellington	P100689 – P100695
Vos, C. Scott, Sqn. Ldr.	P100287
Waterton, William A., Sqn. Ldr.	P100287
Westland Belvedere	P100696 – P100697
Weklin	P100701 – P100705
Wyvern	P100716
Westland-Sikorsky W.S.51 Dragonfly	P100698 – P100697
W.S.55 Whirlwind	P100707 – P100715

Photograph Reference Numbers

P100000(C) – P100002(C)
Airspeed A.S.57 Ambassador (G-AGUA), right front views banking to right; and right front view in flight, 19.2.1948.

P100003(C)
Armstrong Whitworth A.W.27 Ensign (G-ADSU) of BOAC, close-up front left side view.

P100004(C) – P100008(C)
Armstrong Whitworth A.W.55 Apollo (G-AIYN), under rear; front left above; above front left side; above rear left side; and above left side views in flight, 2.9.1949.

P100009(C) – P100010(C)
Gloster Meteors NF.14 (WS805 P, WS788 Z, WS783 T, WS786 F, WS786 F, WS735 X, WS789 R, & WS785 C) and NF.12 (WS690 V, & WS603 A) of No. 152 Sqn, RAF, under rear right side views in formation flight, 14.6.1955.

P100011(C) – P100012(C)
Auster AOP.IV (MT225), close-up right side view of rear fuselage being held up by a woman, Rearsby, 27.3.1944.

P100013(C)
Aviation Traders ATL-41 Accountant (G-ATEL), above front right side view, banking to right, September 1957.

P100014(C) – P100015(C)
Avro XIX Srs. 1 (G-AHXM) of the Sperry Gyroscope Co., front right side; and above front left side views in flight, 1951.

P100016(C)
Avro Anson I, close-up left side of front, being started, RAF North Weald, 1942.

P100017(C) – P100018(C)
Avro Anson T.20 (VS504), above front left side; and front left side views in flight, 9.2.1948.

P100019(C) – P100022(C)
Avro Athena (VM125), above left front banking to left; and front left side views in flight, 27.7.1948.

P100023(C) – P100024(C)
Avro Lancasters I (R5570 EM-F, L7583 EM-A, & another) of No. 207 Sqn, RAF, above rear left side views in formation flight, 20.6.1942.

P100025(C)
Avro Lancaster I (L7538 EM-A) of No. 207 Sqn, RAF, above rear left side view in flight, 20.6.1942.

P100026(C)
Avro Lancaster III (ED592), above rear left side view in flight.

P100027(C)
Avro 691 Lancastrians of Skyways, close-up front left side view being loaded with fuel, Berlin Airlift.

P100034(C) – P100035(C)
Avro 683 Lancaster III (G-AHJV) of Flight Refuelling Ltd, above front left side; and front left side views in flight

P100040(C)
Avro Lincoln B.2 (RF402), de-icing test aircraft, above left side view in flight, July 1956.

P100041(C)
Avro 698 Tudor II (G-AGSU), close-up left side view of nose on ground, Woodford, 27.3.1946.

P100042(C) – P100043(C)
Avro 688 Tudor IV (G-AHNN) of British South American Airways, front left side; and under left front views in flight, 9.2.1948.

P100044(C)
Avro 685 York I (G-AGJA) of BOAC, above rear left side view in flight, 14.1.1944.

P100045(C) – P100048(C)
Beagle 206Y (G-ARXM), front right side; front right above; and above front right side views in flight, 5.9.1963.

P100049(C) – P100050(C)
Bell 47 (NC19H) and Sikorsky S-51, front right side views in formation flight.

P100051(C) – P100053(C)
General Aircraft Universal (WF320), right front above; left side; and above left side views in flight, 7.7.1953.

P100054(C) – P100056(C)
Blackburn Beverley (WZ889), above right front view in flight, 8.7.1953; and right front views banking to right, September 1953.

P100057(C) – P10061(C)
Blackburn Firebrand TF.IV (EK601), front right side; under front right side; close-up front right side; and front right side views, in flight, 3.7.1945.

P100062(C)
Blackburn Firebrands TF.IV (EK601, & EK617), front left side view in formation flight, 3.7.1945.

P100063(C) – P100067(C)
Boeing B-17 Flying Fortress (297976D) of the 709th BS, 447th BG, USAAF. front left side; close-up front left side; above front left side; above front right side; and under right side views in flight.

P100068(C)
Boeing B-17 Flying Fortresses (231225 G, & others) of the 709th BS, 447th BG, USAAF, under rear left side view in formation flight.

P100069(C) – P100070(C)
Boeing KB-29M Superfortress refuelling a Republic F-84 Thunderjet, above rear left side; and left side views in flight, 2.9.1950.

P100071(C) – P100075(C)
Boeing 377 Stratocruiser (G-AKGH) of BOAC, front left side; above front left side; and above left front views in flight, November 1949.

P100076(C) – P100078(C)
Bristol Type 173 (G-ALBN), under left side; left side; and under left side views in flight, 19.9.1952.

P100079(C) – P100080(C)
Bristol Beaufort I (L9878 MW-R) of No. 217 Sqn, RAF, above right front views in flight.

P100081 (C)
Bristol Beauforts I (MW-U, MW-E, & MW-B) of No. 217 Sqn, RAF, right side view in formation flight.

P100082(C) – P100084(C)
Bristol Brigand TF.I (RH754), right front above; right front under; and front right side views in flight, 3.9.1947.

P100085(C) – P100089(C)
Bristol Type 175 Britannia (G-ALBO), above front right side view on ground; and left front above; left front; above right front; and left front views in flight, 1952.

P100090(C) – P100099(C)
Bristol Type 175 Britannia 102 (G-ANBH) of BOAC, above front; front right side; above left front; above right front; above left front; above right front; close-up above left front; and under left front views in flight, 5.7.1955.

P100100(C) – P100103(C)
Bristol Type 175 Britannia 310 (G-ANCA), front right side; and right front under views in flight, September 1957.

P100104(C) – P100106(C)
Bristol Type 170 Freighter Mk.2 (G-AGPV), above left front;l and above rear left side views in flight.

P100107(C) – P100108(C)
Bristol Type 170 Freighter Mk.31 (EI-AFP) of Aer Lingus, under left front; and above front right side views in flight.

P100109(C) – P100112(C)
Bristol Sycamore HC.14 (XG538), front left side; above rear left side; and front left side views in flight, 15.2.1956.

P100113(C)
Hunting Jet Provost T.1 (XD674), above front left side view in flight, 25.8.1954.

P100114(C) – P100116(C)
British Aircraft Corporation Jet Provosts T.3 (XM378 21m, XM351 18, & XM368 3) of No. 2 FTS, RAF, front left side; and above front left side views in formation flight, 22.3.1960.

P100117(C) – P100118(C)
English Electric Lightning T.4 (XL628), left front views in flight, September 1959.

P100119(C) – P100126(C)
Chrislea CH.3 Srs.4 Skyjeep (G-AKVS), left front under; front left side; above left front; left side; above left front; under left front; above front left side; and under front left side views in flight, 28.3.1951.

P100127(C) – P100129(C)
Chrislea CH.3 Srs.2 Super Ace (G-AKFD), above left front; under front left side views in flight, 19.8.1948.

P100130 – P100131(C)
Cierva W.11 Air Horse (VZ724), under left front; and under right front views in flight, September 1949.

P100132(C) – P100135(C)
Convair CV-340 (G-ANVP), Napier Eland, above front left side; and above right front views in flight, July 1956.

P100136(C) – P100139(C)
De Havilland DHC-2 Beaver 1 (G-ALOW), left front; and above left front views in flight, 2.4.1950.

P100140(C) – P100141(C)
De Havilland Chipmunk T.10 (WB550), above front left side; and left above views in flight, 29.9.1949.

P100142(C) – P100144(C)
De Havilland D H 108 (VW120), above front right side; above right front; and front left side views in flight, 12.4.1948.

P100145(C)
De Havilland D.H.104 Dove (G-AGPJ), above left front view in flight, 3.5.1946.

P100146(C) – P100148(C)
De Havilland D.H.104 Dove (G-AGUC), left front above; above left front; and above front left side views in flight, 10.5.1946.

P100149(C)
De Havilland Mosquito IV (DK338) of No. 105 Sqn, RAF, front right side view in flight, 11.12.1942.

P100150(C)
Gp Cpt John William Max Aitken standing in front of his Mosquito, RAF Banff,1945.

P100151(C)
De Havilland Mosquito VI (HR366) of the Wing Leader Banff, left front view running-up prior to take-off, RAF Banff, 1945.

P100152(C) – P100153(C)
De Havilland Mosquito VI (PZ438 NE-) of No. 143 Sqn, front right side views on ground, being loaded with rocket projectiles, RAF Banff, February 1945.

P100154(C) – P100156(C)
De Havilland Mosquito B.XVI (ML963 8K-K) of No. 571 Sqn, RAF, front left side; and above front left side views in flight, 30.9.1944.

P100157(C)
De Havilland Mosquito PR.XVI (NS777) of No. 140 Sqn, RAF, rear left side view on ground, Melsbroek, winter 1944/45.

P100158(C)
De Havilland Mosquito FB.6 (RS650 AK-F) of No. 334 sqn, Norwegian Air Force, above front left side view in flight, June 1949.

P100159(C) – P100160(C)
De Havilland Sea Hornet F.20 (PX212), left front view just landed; and rear right side view on deck of HMS Ocean.

P100161(C) – P100162(C)
De Havilland Sea Hornets FR.20 (TT206 151/FD, TT204 154/FD, & TT211 158/FD) of No. 801 Sqn, FAA, above front right side; and front left side views in formation flight, 27.10.1947.

P100163(C) – P100165(C)
De Havilland Sea Hornet FR.20 (VZ708 456/C) of No. 801 Sqn, FAA, front right side; above front right side; and above right front views in flight over Gibraltar, March 1950.

P100166(C)
De Havilland Sea Mosquito TR.33 (TW256 953/LP) of No. 711 Sqn, FAA, front left side view in flight, 27.10.1947.

P100167(C)
De Havilland D.H.82A Tiger Moth (floatplane) (G-AIVW), left front view at water's edge.

P10068(C)
De Havilland Tiger Moth T.2 of Cambridge University Air Sqn, close-up left side view of nose showing badge, with two pilots standing in front.

P100169(C)
De Havilland D.H.82A Tiger Moth (G-ALND), front right side view in flight over the Solent with RMS Durban Castle below, 1950.

P100170(C)
Sqn Ldr C. Scott Vos of No. 247 Sqn, RAF, standing by the fin of a Vampire F.1 showing badge, RAF Odiham, 25.7.1946.

P100171(C) – P100173(C)
De Havilland Vampire F.I (TG278), under left front; front left side; and above left front side views in flight, 23.8.1945.

P100174(C)
De Havilland Vampires F.3 (VT793 G, & others) of No. 601 sqn, RAaxAF, front right side view in line on ground, Ta Kali, June 1952.

P100175(C)
De Havilland Vampires F.3 (H, & others) of No. 601 Sqn, RAuxAF, front right side view in line on ground, Ta Kali, June 1952.

P100176(C) – P100177(C)
De Havilland Vampire F.3 (AH-B) of No. 332 Sqn, Norwegian Air Force, above front left side views in flight, June 1949.

P100178(C) – P100183(C)
Edgar Percival E.P.9 (G-AOFU), under left front; above left front; front left above; left front; under front left side; and left front views in flight, June 1956.

P100184(C)
English Electric Canberra T.4 (WN467), left front view in flight, 25.9.1952.

P100185(C)
Ercoupe 415 (OO-ERO), above front left side view in flight, 11.5.1947.

P100186(C)
Fairey Barracuda I (P9659), front left side view in flight, May 1943.

P100187(C)
Fairey Barracuda II (P9667), above front left side view in flight, 13.8.1943.

P100188(C)
Fairey Barracudas III (310/GN, & 302/GN) of No. 744 Sqn, FAA, above rear right side view in formation flight, over Skye, 8.3.1949.

P100189(C) – P100190(C)
Blackburn Firebrand TF.IV (EK601), front left above; and above front left side views, in flight, 3.7.1945.

P100191(C) – P100196(C)
Fairey F.D.2 (WG774), right rear under; rear right side; rear right under; under rear left side; and above rear right side views in flight, September 1955.

P100197(C) – P100198(C)
Fairey Firefly F.I (Z1832), right under; and above front left side views in flight, 27.4.1944.

P100199(C) – P100201(C)
Fairey Firefly F.I (Z2035), left front above; and front right side views in flight, 3.5.1944.

P100202(C) – P100203(C)
Fairey Fireflies T.1 (12-11) of the Netherlands Navy and (Z2027), front left side views in formation flight, 2.2.1948.

P100204(C)
Fairey Firefly T.1 (Z2027), above front left side view in flight, 2.2.1948.

P100205(C) – P100206(C)
Fairey Fireflies FR.4 (VH133 227/JR, TW726 228/JR, & TW730 231/JR) of No. 816 Sqn and Hawker Sea Furys FB.10 (TF952 106/JR, VR950 107/JR, & TF925 110/JR) of No. 805 Sqn, Royal Australian Navy, left side views in formation flight, 3.12.1948.

P100207(C)
Fairey Fulmar II (N4040) of No. 761 Sqn, FAA, close-up left side view being manhandled, RNAS Yeovilton, 18.11.1942.

P100208(C) – P100209(C)
Fairey Gannet (VR557), above front right side; and under front right side views in flight, 20.7.1950.

P100210(C) – P100211(C)
Fairey Gannet (WE488), front left side views in flight, 20.7.1950.

P100212(C) – P100215(C)
Fairey Gannet T.2 (WN365), front left side; front right side; and front left side views in flight, 29.9.1955.

P100216(C)
Fairey Gannets AS.1 (WN396 411, WN391 414, WN424 418, & WN419 412) of No. 824 Sqn, FAA, above front right side view in formation flight, 26.4.1955.

P100217(C) – P100219(C)
Fairey Gannet AS.4 (XA425), front left side views in flight, June 1956.

P100220(C) – P100225(C)
Fairey Gyrodyne (G-AIKF), under front right side; under left front; under right front; under left front; under front left side; and under front right side views in flight, White Waltham, June 1948.

P100226(C) – P100228(C)
Fairey Primer (G-ALBL), above front left side; and front left side views in flight, 25.11.1948.

P100229(C) – P100231(C)
Fairey Primer (OO-POM), front right side; and above front right side views in flight.

P100232(C)
Airspeed A.S.57 Ambassador (G-AGUA), left front view in flight banking to left, 19.2.1948.

P100233(C)
Avro Lancaster I (PP687), left front view in flight.

P100234(C)– P100235(C)
Avro 688 Tudor (G-AHNN) of British South American Airways, above front left side views in flight, 9.2.1948.

P100236(C)
Avro 685 York I (G-AFJA) of BOAC, above rear left side view in flight, 14.1.1944.

P100237(C) – P100238(C)
Blackburn Beverley C.1 (XB283 G) of No. 47 Sqn, RAF, above front left side views in flight, November 1956.

P100239(C)
Hunting Jet Provost T.1 (XD674), front left side view in flight, 25.8.1954.

P100240(C)
British Aircraft Corporation Jet Provosts T.4 of the CFS "Pelicans", RAF, under left front view in formation flight, Farnborough, September 1962.

P100241(C)
De Havilland DHC-1 Chipmunk, under left front view in flight.

P100242(C)
De Havilland DHC-6 Twin Otter (CF-UXE), left side view about to land, Farnborough, September 1966

P100243(C) – P100245(C)
English Electric Canberra (VN799), above left front; above right front; and right front views in flight, 23.8.1949.

P100246(C) – P100252(C)
English Electric Canberra B.2 (VX165), front right side; above front left side; close-up above front; front left above; above right front; and above front views in flight, 20.7.1950.

P100253(C)
English Electric Canberra PR.3 (WE146), above front right side view in flight, 20.7.1950.

P100254(C)
English Electric Canberra T.4 (WN467), above left front view in flight, 25.9.1952.

P100255(C) – P100257(C)
English Electric Canberras B.2 (WH924, & WH922) of No. 61 Sqn, and (WH741) of No. 109 Sqn, RAF, left front above views in flight, July 1955.

P100258(C)
Fairey Firefly I (Z1980), left front view just landed on aircraft carrier.

P100259(C) – P100261(C)
Fairey Firefly IV (Z2118), under front left side; and above front left side views in flight.

P100262(C)
Fairey Firefly AS.5 (VT406), front right under view in flight.

P100263(C) – P100269(C)
Fairey Rotodyne (XE531), under front left side; front right side; above front right side views, May 1958; and front right side; right front above views in flight.

P100270(C) – P100272(C)
Fairey Swordfish (G-AJVH), Fairey Fulmar II (G-AIBE) and Fairey Gannet AS.4 (XA425), right side views in formation flight, June 1956.

P100273(C) – P100274(C)
Folland Midge (G-39-1), right side; and above right side views in flight, 27.8.1954.

P100275(C)
General Aircraft Hamilcar, close-up left front view on ground with a Bren Carrier in the entrance, RAF Tarrant Rushton, 12.10.1944.

P100276(C) – P100277(C)
General Aircraft Hamilcars, close-up above rear; and left rear views in long line on ground, RAF Tarrant Rushton, 12.10.1944

P100278(C)
Gloster Meteor F.III (EE275 YQ-Q) of No. 616 Sqn, AuxAF, front left side view on ground, Germany, April 1945.

P100279(C) – P100280(C)
Gloster Meteor F.III (EE274 YQ-P) of No. 616 Sqn, AuxAF, front left side; and left front views on ground, Germany, April 1945.

P100281(C) – P100282(C)
Gloster Meteor F.4 (EE528), left side views on ground.

P100283(C) – P100284(C)
Gloster Meteor F.4 (EE521), front right side views in flight.

P100285(C) – P100286(C)
Gloster Meteor I (Trent) (EE227), above front left side; and front left above views in flight, 9.7.1947.

P100287(C)
Sqn Ldr William A. Waterton standing in the cockpit of a Meteor F.4.

P100288(C)
Gloster Meteor F.IV (EE455), close-up right side view of nose showing markings, on ground, 1945.

P100289(C)
Avro Lancaster III (G-33-2), front left side view refuelling Gloster Meteor F.3 (EE397) in flight, 6.8.1949.

P100290(C) –P100294(C)
Gloster Meteor F.3 (EE397), above front; and close-up above front views refuelling from a Lancaster in flight, 6.8.1949.

P100295(C)
Avro Lancaster III (G-33-2), left front view in flight, refuelling Gloster Meteor F.3 (EE397), 6.8.1949.

P100296(C) – P100297(C)
Gloster Meteor F.3 (EE337), left front; and right front views on deck of HMS Implacable, May 1948.

P100298(C)
Gloster Meteors F.4 (VT124, VT125, & RA457) of No. 245 Sqn and (VT111 HE) of No. 263 Sqn, RAF, right side view in line on ground, RAF Horsham St. Faith, 27.4.1948.

P100299(C) – (P10030(C)
Gloster Meteor IV (G-AIDC), above left side; above left front; and above front left side views in flight, 12.4.1947.

P1000302(C)
Gloster Meteor 7 (G-AKPK), front left side view in flight, 13.5.1948.

P100303(C) – P100308(C)
Gloster Meteors F.4 (VZ389) of the Refuelling Flt, and F.8 (WA826 F, & WA829 A) of No. 245 Sqn, RAF, above left side; above rear left side; and under rear left side views in flight, refuelling from Boeing KB-29M Superfortress of the USAF, July 1951.

P100309(C)
Gloster Meteor T.7 left front view taxying Ta Kali, 1952.

P100310(C) – P100311(C)
Gloster Meteors F.8 (WH364 B, WK739 D, WF744 G, & others) or No. 601 Sqn, and others of No. 604 Sqn, RAuxAF, in lines on ground with personnel, RAF North Weald, 20.9.1953.

P100312(C) – P100313(C)
Grumman Avengers I (FN908 4M, FN868 4F, & another) of No. 846 Sqn, FAA, above front right side views in formation flight, 10.12.1943.

P100314(C)
Grumman Wildcat V (JV377 6C) of No. 882 Sqn, FAA, about to take-off from HMS Searcher, 1944.

P100315(C)
Grumman Wildcat V (JV379 6H) of No. 882 Sqn, FAA, left front view on deck of HMS Searcher, 1944.

P100316(C)
Grumman Wildcat V (JV445 6Q) of No. 882 Sqn, FAA, left front view on deck of HMS Searcher, 1944.

P100317(C)
Handley Page Halifax II (W7676 TL-P) of No. 35 Sqn, RAF, above rear left side view in flight, 1942.

P100318(C)
Handley Page Halifaxes II (W7676 TL-P, & TL-F) of No. 35 Sqn, RAF, above left rear view in flight, 1942.

P100319(C)
Handley Page Halifax II of No. 35 Sqn, RAF, close-up view of engines on right side with fitters working on them, RAF Linton-on-Ouse, 1942.

P100320(C)
Handley Page Halifax GT.V (8A-) of No. 298 Sqn, RAF, rear left side view taxying, RAF Tarrant Rushton, 12.10.1944.

P100321(C)
Handley Page Halifax II (W7676 TL-P) of No. 35 Sqn, RAF, rear left above view in flight, 1942.

P100322(C) –P100323(C)
Handley Page Halifax C.VIII (PP285), above rear left side; and above front right side views in flight, 16.5.1945.

P100324(C) – P100325(C)
Handley Page Hampden I (AT137 UB-T) of No. 455 Sqn, RAAF, front right side; and above front right side views in flight, 1942.

P100326(C) – P100327(C)
Handley Page Hastings (TE580), above left front views in flight, 23.5.1946.

P100328(C)
Handley Page Hastings C.1 (TG500), left front view on ground, engines running, Farnborough, 5.7.1950.

P100329(C)
Handley Page Hastings C.1, left front under view dropping supply containers at air display, Farnborough, 5.7.1950.

P100330(C)
Handley Page H.P.R.3 Herald (G-AODE), above front left side view in flight, August 1955.

P100331(C) – P100334(C)
Handley Page H.P.R.3 Herald (G-AODE), above front left side; close-up left side of front; and above front left side views on ground, May 1956.

P100335(C)
Handley Page H.P.82 Hermes 5 (G-ALEU), under left front view in flight at air display, Farnborough, September 1949.

P100336(C) – P100338(C)
Handley Page H.P.82 Hermes 5 (G-ALEV), left front; and close-up front left side views on ground, being refuelled, Berlin Airlift.

P100339(C) – P100343(C)
Handley Page H.P.81 Hermes 4 (G-ALDA) of Airwork Ltd., front left side; and above front left side views in flight, 5.3.1954.

P100344(C)
Handley Page Marathon (VX229), left front above view in flight, 22.7.1952.

P100345(C) – P100347(C)
Handley Page Victor (WB771), under right rear; above right side; and above rear right side views in flight, 10.7.1953.

P100348(C) – P100351(C)
Handley Page Victor B.1 (XA917), above right front; and right front views in flight, September 1956.

P100352(C) – P100357(C)
Handley Page Victor B.1 (XA918), above right front; above front right side; left front above; and above right front views in flight, January 1957.

P100358(C) – P100359(C)
Handley Page Victor B.1 (XA930), left front above; and front left above views in flight, 27.8.1958.

P100360(C) – P100361(C)
Hawker Hurricane I (Z4791 H-33) and Supermarine Spitfires IIa (P7926 3, & P7882) of the ECFS, RAF, front left side views in formation flight.

P100362(C)
Hawker Hurricane IIC (BE500 LK-A) of No. 87 Sqn, RAF, front right side view in flight, 1942.

P100363(C)
Hawker Hurricane IIc (KX193), above left front view in flight, 11.8.1943.

P100364(C) – P100367(C)
Hawker P.1040 (VP401), left front; close-up front; and above left front views in flight, 24.8.1948.

P100368(C) – P100372(C)
Hawker P.1052 (VX279), front left above; above front left side; and above left rear views in flight, 22.4.1949.

P100373(C) – P100379(C)
Hawker P.1052 (VX279), close-up above left front; above front left side; above right front; left above; above left front; and left above views in flight, 28.6.1949

P100380(C) – P100381(C)
Hawker Sea Fury T.20 (VX818), left front above; and above left front views in flight, January 1949.

P100382(C) – P100385(C)
Hawker Sea Hawks FB.3 of No. 738 Sqn, FAA, right front above; above right front; and under right front views in formation flight, trailing smoke, August 1958.

P100386(C) – P100387(C)
Hawker Sea Hurricane IA (P3090 W8-E) of No. 760 Sqn, FAA, front right side; and right side views in flight, 18.11.1942.

P100388(C)
Hawker Sea Hurricane IB (Z4039) of No. 760 Sqn, RAF, above front right side view in flight, 18.11.1942.

P100389(C)
Hawker Tempest V (EJ7-- SD-) of No. 501 Sqn, AuxAF, right front view taxying, RAF Bradwell Bay, 18.10.1944.

P100390(C) – P100391(C)
Hawker Tempest V (NV696), above right front; and front right side views in flight, 25.11.1944.

P100392(C) – P100393(C)
Hawker Tempest II (MW764), front right side views in flight, 22.3.1945.

P100394(C) – P100397(C)
Hawker Tempest II (PR533), front right side; front left side; and above front right side views in flight, 19.7.1945.

P100398(C)
Hawker Tempest V (NV768), above front left side view in flight, 12.7.1946.

P100399(C) – P100401(C)
Hawker Typhoon IB (EK183 US-A) of No. 56 Sqn, RAF, rear left side; and close-up left front views on ground, RAF Matlask, 21.4.1943.

P100402(C)
Hawker Typhoon IB No. 257 Sqn, RAF, close-up of engine with fitters working on it, RAF Warmwell, 13.5.1943.

P100403(C)
Hawker Typhoon IB (FM-L) of No. 257 Sqn, RAF, close-up front left side view with armourers loading guns, RAF Warmwell, 13.5.1943.

P100404(C) – P100406(C)
Hawker Typhoon IB (EK172 FM-M) of No. 257 Sqn, RAF, close-up right side view of cockpit with a Sgt pilot in it; close-up right side view of front, starting up; and close-up right front view with pilots in front, RAF Warmwell, 13.5.1943.

P100407(C)
Hawker Typhoon IB (EJ927 FM-) of No. 257 Sqn, RAF, front left side view on ground, RAF Warmwell, 13.5.1943.

P100408(C)
Hawker Typhoon IB (JP682), front left side view in flight, 24.8.1943.

P100409(C) – P100410(C)
Hawker Typhoon IB (MN686), right front; and above right front views in flight, 1944.

P100411(C)
Hawker Siddeley A.W.650 Argosy 102 (G-APRN), front left side view taxying, Farnborough, 1960.

P100412(C)
Blackburn Buccaneer (XK486), left side view in flight, 23.10.1958.

P100413(C) P100414(C)
Blackburn Buccaneer (XK490), right side; and front right above views in flight, September 1959.

P100415(C)
Blackburn Buccaneer S.1 (XN921 119/R) of No. 801 Sqn, FAA, above right front view in flight, September 1962.

P100416(C) – P100417(C)
De Havilland D.H.106 Comet 1 (G-ALVG), left front under; and front left side views in flight, November 1949.

P100418(C)
Hawker Siddeley D.H.106 Comet 1A (CF-CUM), above front view in flight, 2.4.1951.

P100419(C) – P100424(C)
Hawker Siddeley Comet C.2 (XK695) of No. 216 Sqn, RAF, front left side views in flight, 20.11.1956.

P100425(C)
Hawker Siddeley Comet 4C (OD-ADR) of Middle East Airlines, front right side view in flight, 1961.

P100426(C)
Hawker Siddeley Comet 4C (OD-ADQ) of Middle East Airlines, front left side view on ground, Beirut, 1961.

P100427(C) – P100431(C)
Folland Gnat (G-39-2), above right front; front right side; front right above; above rear right side; and front right side views in flight, 25.8.1955.

P100432(C)
De Havilland D.H.125 (G-ARYA), right side view in flight, September 1962.

P100433(C) – P100434(C)
Hawker Hunter 3 (WB188), above left front; and close-up above right front views with Neville Duke standing in front, Dunsfold, 19.9.1953.

P100435(C)
Hawker Hunters F.2 (WN950 F, WN915 T, WN948 R, & WN952 G) of No. 257 Sqn, RAF, under right side view in formation flight, 14.4.1955.

P100436(C)
Hawker Hunter F.2 of No. 257 Sqn, RAF, close-up front right side view in flight, 14.4.1955.

P100437(C)
Hawker Hunters F.2 (WN950 F, WN915 T, WN948 R, & WN952 G) of No. 257 Sqn, RAF, rear right under view in formation flight, 14.4.1955.

P100438(C)
Hawker Hunters F.2 (WN915 T, & others) of No. 257 Sqn, RAF, rear right under view in formation flight, 14.4.1955.

P100439(C) – P100440(C)
Hawker Hunters F.2 (WN915 T, & WN948 R) of No. 257 Sqn, RAF, rear right under; and under right side views in formation flight, 14.4.1955.

P100441(C) – P100442(C)
Hawker Hunters F.2 of No. 257 Sqn, RAF, above rear left side views in squadron formation flight, 14.4.1955.

P100443(C)
Hawker Hunters F.6 of No. 111 Sqn, RAF, aerobatic formation over control tower, Farnborough, September 1960.

P100444(C)
Hawker Hunters F.6 of No. 92 Sqn, RAF, aerobatic formation over airfield, Farnborough, September 1962.

P100445(C)
Hawker P.1127 (XP972) and Hawker Hunter T.66A (G-APUX), above front right side view in formation flight, September 1962.

P100446(C)
Hawker P.1127 (XP972), above right front view banking to right, September 1962.

P100447(C) – P100452(C)
Avro Shackleton (VW135), above front left side; under front left side; front left side; above front left side; front left side; and under front left side views in flight, 18.4.1950.

P100453(C)
Avro Shackleton MR.2 (WG531), above front left side view in fight, September 1952.

P100454(C) – P100455(C)
Hawker Siddeley H.S.121 Trident 1 (G-ARPC) of BEA, front right side views in flight, September 1962.

P100456(C) – P100460(C)
Avro Vulcan (VX770), left front above; above front left side; left front above; left under; and above front left side views in flight, September 1952.

P100461(C)
Avro Vulcan, above right front view in flight.

P100462(C)
Junkers Ju 87D-7 of the Luftwaffe, left front view on ground, with Ju 88 (--+EU) right rear view in background, 1945.

P100463(C) – P100464(C)
Douglas DC-2 of the South African Air Force, close-up right front views on ground.

P100465(C) – P100467(C)
Lockheed Hudsons III (V9029 OD-J, V9032 OD-N, & V8986 OD-K) of No. 6 (C)OTU, RAF, front left side; under left front; and above front left side views in formation flight, 15.12.1941.

P100468(C)
Miles Master I of No. 760 Sqn, FAA, close-up left front view being refuelled from bowser, RNAS Yeovilton, 18.11.1942.

P100469(C) – P100470(C)
Martin B-26B Marauder (296142 X2-A) of the 397th BG, 596th BS, USAAF, left front above; and above front left side views in flight, August 1944.

P100471(C)
Miles M.57 Aerovan 1 (G-AGOZ), left front view in flight, banking to left, 17.6.1947.

P100472(C)
Miles M.57 Aerovan 4 (G-AJTD), front left side view in flight, banking to left, 17.6.1947.

P100473(C) – P100474(C)
Miles M.57 Aerovan 1 (G-AGOZ), left front; and front left side views in flight, 17.6.1947.

P100475(C)
Miles M.57 Aerovan 4 (G-AJTD), above front left side view in flight, 17.6.1947.

P100476(C)
Miles HDM 105 (G-AHDM), above front right side view in flight, 11.9.1957.

P100477(C) – P100478(C)
Miles M.65 Gemini 1 (G-AGUS), above front left side views in flight, 11.2.1946

P100479(C) – P100480(C)
Miles M.65 Gemini 1A (G-AISM), above front left side; and front left side views in flight, 17.6.1947.

P100481(C) – P100482(C)
Miles Martinet TT.1 (HN862), front left side views in flight.

P100483(C)
Miles M.38 Messenger 3 (G-AGOY), above right front view in flight, banking to right, 17.5.1946.

P100484(C) – P100485(C)
Miles M.38 Messenger 2A (G-AJEY), above front right side views in flight, 17.6.1947.

P100486(C) – P100487(C)
Mitchell-Proctor Kittiwake 1 (G-ATZN), front left side views in flight.

P100488(C)
North American Mitchells II (FL684 EV-S, FL707 EV-Z, & others) of No. 180 Sqn, RAF, front left side view in line on ground, RAF Foulsham, 28.7.1943.

P100489(C)
North American Mitchell II (FL218 EV-W) of No. 180 Sqn, RAF, close-up left side view of nose, with another (FL685 EV-) behind, RAF Foulsham, 28.7.1943.

P100490(C)
North American Mitchell II (EV-) of No. 180 Sqn, RAF, rear left side view, nose in a barn, Melsbroek, 1944.

P100491(C)
North American Mitchell II (EV-P) of No. 180 Sqn, RAF, left side view being dismantled, Melsbroek, 1944.

P100492(C) – P100495(C)
North American Mustang I (AG550 XV-U) of No. 2 Sqn, RAF, close-up left side view of cockpit; close-up of left front views, engine running; and front left side view taxying, RAF Sawbridgeworth, 24.7.1942.

P100496(C)
North American Mustang I (AG633 XV-E) of No. 2 Sqn, RAF, above front left side view in flight, 24.7.1942.

P100497(C) – P100498(C)
Northrop P-61A Black Widow (25565) of the 422nd NFS, USAAF, above front left side; and front left above views in flight, 28.8.1944.

P100499(C)
Percival Prentice (TV163), front right side view in flight, 27.5.1946.

P100500(C) – P100501(C)
Percival Prentice of the Argentinian Air Force, front right side; and above right front views in flight, 8.4.1949.

P100502(C) – P100503(C)
Percival P.50 Prince 1 (G-ALJA), above left front; and left front views in flight, 10.8.1949.

P100504(C) – P100507(C)
Percival Proctor IV (LA589), above front right side; front left side; under front left side; and under left front views in flight, 10.8.1943.

P100508(C)
Percival Proctors IV (NP229, LA586, & others) and III (DX193), above front right side view in line on ground, Luton, 12.4.1944.

P100509(C) – P100510(C)
Percival Proctor IV (LA586), above left front views in flight, 12.4.1944.

P100511(C)
Percival P.44 Proctors 5 (CS-ADN, & G-AGSW) front left side view in formation flight, 30.10.1945.

P100512(C)
Percival P.44 Proctor 5 (CS-ADN), above front left side view in flight, 30.10.1945.

P100513(C) – P100515(C)
Percival Provost (WE522), above front right side; close-up left side of front; and left front views in flight, 21.5.1952.

P100516(C) – P100519(C)
Piaggio P.166 (I-PIAK), right front; and front right side views in flight, April 1959.

P100520(C) – P100521(C)
Republic P-47C Thunderbolt of the 56th FG, USAAF, close-up left front; and left front views taxying.

P100522(C) – P100525(C)
Saro SR.A/1 (TG263), under front right side; above front left side; and front left side views in flight, 29.7.1947.

P100526(C)
Saro SR.45 Princess (G-ALUN), under left front view in flight, Farnborough, September 1953.

P100527(C) – P100532(C)
Scottish Aviation Twin Pioneer (G-ANTP), front right side; above right front; right front; and above front right side views in flight, 17.8.1955.

P100533(C)
Scottish Aviation Twin Pioneer (G-APLW), right front view in flight, 22.7.1958.

P100534(C) – P100535(C)
Scottish Aviation Twin Pioneer CC.1 (XM286), front left side; and above front left side views in flight, 22.7.1958.

P100536(C)
Scottish Aviation Twin Pioneer (G-APPH), under left front view in flight, Farnborough, September 1960.

P100537(C) – P100538(C)
Short Belfast C.1 (XR364), left front; and rear right side views taxying, Farnborough, September 1964.

P100539(C) – P100541(C)
Short S.B.5 (WG768), above left front; left front above; and above left front views in flight, May 1953.

P100542(C) – P100543(C)
Short S.C.1 (XG905), under left side views descending in front of hangar, Bedford, 13.7.1960.

P100544(C)
Short S.C.1 (XG905), under rear left side view in flight, Farnborough, September 1960.

P100545(C) – P100547(C)
Short S.44 Sealand 1 (G-AKLM), above front right side; front right side; and above right front views in flight, 26.9.1949.

P100548(C) – P100549(C)
Short Shetland I (DZ166), above front left side views in flight, 31.5.1945.

P100550(C) – P100553(C)
Short S.45A Solent 2 (G-AHIY) of BOAC, front left side view in flight; right front view taxying on water, Rochester; front left side view in flight; and above right front view in flight, 9.4.1948.

P100554(C)
Short S.45A Solent 2 (G-AHIN) of BOAC, above rear right side view in flight over Southampton Docks, 22.5.1948.

P100555(C)
Short S.45A Solent 2 (G-AHIS) of BOAC, under rear right side view in flight, September 1948.

P100556(C)
Short Stirling I (N3676 S) of No. 1651 HCU, RAF, close-up left rear view with aircrew in front, RAF Waterbeach, 29.4.1942.

P100557(C)
Group photograph of some aircrew of No. 1651 HCU, RAF, under the nose of a Stirling I, RAF Waterbeach, 29.4.1942.

P100558(C) – P100565(C)
Short Stirling I (N6101 E) of No. 1651 HCU, RAF, front right side; close-up front right side; close-up right side of nose; close-up front left side; and clos-up views of nose and engines, RAF Waterbeach, 29.4.1942.

P100566(C) – P100567(C)
Short Stirling I of No. 1651 HCU, RAF, close-up views of rear turret with gunner in position, RAF Waterbeach, 29.4.1942.

P100568(C) – P100570(C)
Short Stirling I of No. 1651 HCU, RAF, interior views of cockpit with crew in position, RAF Waterbeach, 29.4.1942.

P100571(C) – P100574(C)
Short Stirlings I (N3676 S, N6096 C, & G) of No. 1651 HCU, RAF, above rear right side views in flight, 9.4.1942.

P100575(C)
Short Stirlings I (N3676 S, & G) of No. 1651 HCU, RAF, close-up above rear right side view in formation flight, 9.4.1942.

P100576(C)
Short Stirling IV (V8-C) of No. 570 Sqn, RAF, rear left side view taxying, with a Sgt with a signal lamp and parasol in foreground, 1954.

P100577(C) – P100578(C)
Short Sturgeon I (RK791), left rear views landing on deck of HMS Implacable, 16.6.1948.

P100579(C) – P100580(C)
Short Sunderland MR.5 (PP117 4X-W) of No. 230 Sqn, RAF, above front left side views in flight, March 1950.

P100581(C) – P100582(C)
Short S.25 Sunderland III (G-AGJM), front right side views in flight, 6.11.1946.

P100583(C)
Sikorsky Hoverfly II (KN846) of the Airborne Forces Experimental Establishment, made up as a pink elephant at air display, front left side view about to land, RAF Beaulieu, 19.6.1950.

P100584(C) – P100585(C)
Supermarine Type 510 (VV106), left front above; and above left front views in flight, 10.8.1949.

P100586(C) – P100587(C)
Supermarine Attackers F.1 (WA496 101, WA494 105, & WA479 102) of No. 800 Sqn, FAA, front left side views in flight, 1951.

P100588(C) – P100590(C)
Supermarine Attacker F.1 (WA5--) of No. 800 Sqn, FAA, under left front views landing on HMS Eagle, 5.6.1952.

P100591(C)
Supermarine Seafire IIC of No. 760 Sqn, FAA, close-up view of left side of cockpit and forward fuselage with personnel looking in, RNAS Yeovilton, 18.11.1942.

P100592(C)
Supermarine Seafires IIC (MB217, & MB264) and Hawker Sea Hurricane IB (Z4039) of No. 760 Sqn, FAA, front right side view in formation flight, 18.11.1942.

P100593(C)
Supermarine Seafire F.15 (SR572), under front view coming in to land on carrier, 1951.

P100594(C) – P100595(C)
Supermarine Seagull (S.14/44) (PA143), left side; and under left side views in flight, 19.10.1948.

P100596(C) – P100598(C)
Supermarine Spiteful F.XIV (RB515), above left front; and above front left side views in flight, 27.7.1945.

P100599(C) – P100600(C)
Supermarine Spitfire VB (BM202 ZD-H) of No. 222 Sqn, RAF, close-up left side view of foreward fuselage with pilot being strapped in; and close-up left side view of foreward fuselage starting up, RAF North Weald, 4.5.1942.

P100601(C)
Supermarine Spitfire VB (AD233 ZD-F) of No. 222 Sqn, RAF, above front right side view in flight, 4.5.1942.

P100602(C) – P100604(C)
Supermarine Spitfire VB (BL479 SZ-X) of No. 316 (Polish) Sqn, RAF, front right side; and rear right under views in flight, 6.8.1943.

P100605(C)
Supermarine Spitfires I (AR238 F, K9969, R7193, & X4643) of No. 761 Sqn, FAA, front right side view in formation flight, 18.11.1942.

P100606(C) – P100608(C)
Supermarine Spitfire PR.XI (EN654), front left side; and above front left side views in flight, 17.10.1943.

P100609(C)
Supermarine Spitfire XIVE, close-up right front view on ground, engine being serviced.

P100610(C) – P100612(C)
Supermarine Spitfire XIVC, close-up left front; and left front views on ground, engine running.

P100613(C)
Supermarine Spitfires F.XXI (LA232, & LA217) and F.22 (PK312), front above view in formation flight, March 1945.

P100616(C) – P100619(C)
Supermarine Spitfire VIII (2-seat) (N32), under front left side; and front left side views in flight, 24.1.1947.

P100620(C) – P100623(C)
Supermarine Swift (WJ960), right front above; front right above; and right side views in flight, August 1951.

P100624(C)
Tipsy Trainer 1 (G-AFSC), above front right side view in flight, 10.5.1950.

P100625(C) – P100626(C)
Tipsy Belfair (OO-TIA) front right side; and left front above views in flight, 28.4.1947.

P100627(C) – P100629(C)
Vickers Valetta C.1 (VL263), front right side; left front; and above front right side views in flight, 2.2.1949.

P100630(C) – P100631(C)
Vickers Valiant (WB210), above front left side; and above left views in flight, August 1951.

P100632(C) – P100635(C)
Vickers Valiant (WB215), above front left side; front left side; left side; and above left front views in flight, 25.9.1953.

P100636(C)
Vickers Valiant B.2 (WJ954), above front view in flight, 11.9.1953.

P100637(C)
Vickers V.951 Vanguard (G-APEB) of BEA, right front under view banking to left, September 1959.

P100638(C) – P100639(C)
Vickers V.952 Vanguard (CF-TKB) of Trans-Canada Airlines, left front; and right front views taxiing, 1961.

P100640(C) – P100644(C)
Vickers Varsity (VX828), above front right side; above front left side; and front left side views in flight, 10.9.1949.

P100645(C) – P100648(C)
Vickers V.495 Viking 1 (G-AGOL), left side; above left front; and above front left side views in flight, 19.9.1945.

P100649(C) – P100650(C)
Vickers V.498 Viking 1A (G-AGON), above front left side; and front left side views in flight, 30.4.1946.

P100651(C) – P100652(C)
Vickers V.604 Viking 1B (VT-AZA) of Indian National Airways, above rear left side; and above front left side views in flight, 11.8.1946.

P100653(C) – P100655(C)
Vickers Viking C.2 (VL246), front right side; and under front right side views in flight, 29.1.1947.

P100656(C) – P100661(C)
Vickers V.636 Viking 1B (G-AJJN), above front left side; above left front; above left side; left above; and above front left side views in flight, 10.4.1947.

P100662(C) – P100664(C)
Vickers V.641 Viking 1 (VP-YHJ) of Central African Airways, right side; above front right side; and front right above views in flight, 6.9.1947.

P100665(C) – P100667(C)
Vickers V.618 Viking (Nene) (G-AJPH), above front right side; and right side views in flight, 24.6.1948.

P100668(C) – P100673(C)
Vickers V.630 Viscount (VX211), under front right side; above front right side; front right side; and under right front views in flight, 10.8.1949.

P100674(C) – P100675(C)
Vickers V.700 Viscount (G-AMAV) of BEA, front left side views in flight, September 1951.

P100676(C)
Vickers V.701 Viscount (G-ALWE) of BEA, above front left side view in flight, September 1952.

P100677(C) – P100679(C)
Vickers V.744 Viscount (N7402) of Capital Airlines, above front right side views in flight, 31.5.1955.

P100680(C) – P100681(C)
Vickers V.803 Viscount (PH-VID) of KLM, front right side views in flight, September 1957.

P100682(C) – P100683(C)
Vickers Type 456 Warwick I (G-AGFK) of BOAC, above front left side; and above left front views in flight, 13.7.1943.

P100684(C) – P100686(C)
Vickers Warwick ASR.I (BV285), above front left side; and left front under views in flight, 13.7.1943.

P100687(C) – P100688(C)
Vickers Warwick GR.V (PN811 OZ-V) of No. 179 Sqn, RAF, left side; and right front above views in flight, 15.12.1945.

P100689(C) – P100691(C)
Vickers Wellington III of No. 419 Sqn, RCAF, close-up right front views on ground, about to be loaded with a 4,000lb bomb, RAF Mildenhall, 27.5.1942.

P100692(C) – P100694(C)
Vickers Wellington III (Z1572 VR-Q) of No. 419 Sqn, RCAF, above front left side; above front right side; and front right above views in flight, 27.5.1942.

P100695(C)
Vickers Wellington IA (N2887 5) of the Central Gunnery School, RAF, above front left side view in flight, 24.6.1943.

P100696(C) – P100697(C)
Westland Belvedere HC.1 (XG447), above rear left side views in flight.

P100698(C)
Westland Sikorsky W.S.51 Mk.1A (G-ALEI), left front view crop spraying in Normandy, 9.6.1949.

P100699(C) – P100700(C)
Westland-Sikorsky W.S.51 Mk.1A (G-AKTW), above front right side views in flight, 2.4.1952.

P100701(C) – P100705(C)
Westland Welkin I (DX318), right front; above right front; and above front right side views in flight, 20.4.1944.

P100706(C)
Sikorsky S-58 (XL722), rear right side view in flight, September 1957.

P100707(C)
Westland Whirlwind I (P7048), above front left side view in flight, 20.4.1944.

P100708(C) – P100709(C)
Westland W.S.55 (G-ANJT) and Westland Whirlwind HAR.1 (XA866), front left side; and front right side views in formation flight, 24.6.1956.

P100710(C) – P100713(C)
Westland W.S.55 (G-ANJT), rear right side; above rear right side; right side; and above front right side views in flight, 24.6.1956.

P100714(C) – P100715(C)
Westland W.S.55 (G-ANJT) and Westland Whirlwind HAR.1 (XA866), right side; and under front left side views in flight, 24.6.1956.

P100716(C)
Westland Wyverns S.4 of No. 813 Sqn, FAA, under rear left side view of six in formation flight, 25.8.1953.

P100717(C)
Bristol Type 175 Britannia 301 (G-ANCA), under front right side view in flight, September 1957.

P100718(C)
Blackburn Firebrands IV (EK617, & EK601), above front left side; and front left side views in flight, 3.7.1945.

P100719(C) – P100722(C)
Blackburn Firebrand IV (EK601), under left front; front right side; under left front; and front right side views in flight, 3.7.1945.

P100723(C) – P100728(C)
Boeing B-17G Flying Fortress (297976 D) of the 709th BS, 447th BG, USAAF, rear left under; above front right side; and close-up above front right side views in flight.

P100729(C)
Fairey Firefly AS.5 (VT---), under left front view about to land on an aircraft carrier.

P100730(C) – P100731(C)
Gloster Meteor F.4 (EE455), close-up right side views of nose showing markings, 1945.

P100732(C)
Slingsby Type 25 Gull 4, above front left side view in flight.

P100733(C)
Slingsby Type 41 Skylark 2, right front view in flight, July 1955.

P100734(C)
Slingsby Type 45 Swallow (80), under rear left side view in flight, July 1959.

P100735(C)
Slingsby Type 43 Skylark 3G (13), above left front view in flight.

P100736(C) – P100737(C)
Slingsby Type 50 Skylark 4, front left above; and above right front views in flight.

P100738(C) – P100739(C)
Slingsby Type 49 Capstan, above left front views in flight, 15.9.1963.

P100740(C) – P100743(C)
Slingsby Type 51 Dart 17 (32), above left front; and above front left side views in flight.

P100744(C) – P100746(C)
Standard Austria, above left front views in flight, May 1964.

P100747(C) – P100751(C)
68' High Speed Launch No. 2626 of the Royal Air Force, right front; front; and rear left side views at speed.

P100752(C) – P100755(C)
HMS Bulwark, right front views at sea; and above rear right side view leaving Portsmouth, 1956.

P100756(C)
HMS Bulwark, above left front view at sea, 1960.

P100757(C)
HMS Implacable, above front left side view at sea.

P100758(C) – P100760(C)
Air Chief Marshal Sir William Dickson, portrait photographs.

P100761(C)
Geoffrey de Havilland in the cockpit of a Vampire.

P100762(C)
A.W. (Bill) Bedford in the cockpit of a Tempest.

P100763(C)
P.E.G. Sayer standing in the cockpit of a Tempest.

P100764(C)
Flt Lt W.V. Crawford-Compton of No. 611 Sqn, AuxAF, in the cockpit of a Spitfire IXC, RAF Biggin Hill, 8.12.1942.

P100765(C)
Sqn Ldr H.T.Armstrong of No. 611 Sqn, AuxAF, in the cockpit of a Spitfire IXC, RAF Biggin Hill, 8.12.1942.